Original title:
Vineyard Verses

Copyright © 2025 Creative Arts Management OÜ
All rights reserved.

Author: Sophia Kingsley
ISBN HARDBACK: 978-1-80566-688-2
ISBN PAPERBACK: 978-1-80566-973-9

The Cherished Crush

In a land of grapes, so round and sweet,
I tripped on a vine, fell right at your feet.
You laughed so hard, you nearly fell too,
My face turned as red as the wine that we brew.

The sun was shining, the birds did sing,
You whispered, "Is that a grape or a ring?"
I tried to be smooth, but failed with a fumble,
You said, "Don't worry, I like a good stumble!"

As we stomped the fruit, our feet all a-squish,
I made a joke about making a wish.
You said, "Only if it's to crush more of these!"
I grinned and thought, that's the best of cheer!

So here's to the laughs, amidst grape vines so fine,
To moments that sparkle like our favorite wine.
With jokes and with clumsiness, love's in the air,
In this fruity affair, we've little to spare!

Shadows and Sips

In the shade, a bottle waits,
Sunlight beams on clinking plates.
Grapes are laughing, rolling free,
Whispering secrets, just like me.

Beneath the leaves, we share a joke,
The cork pops loud, the tension broke.
Sipping slowly, we toast to fun,
And laugh at how the grapes all run.

Crescendo of the Cork

The cork is primed, the moment's grand,
Pop it high, let laughter stand.
A foamy splash, then playful whim,
As glasses clink, we sing our hymn.

Grapes are dancing, rolling loose,
They giggle more when we let loose.
Pour another, the fun's a whirl,
In our world, the bottles swirl.

The Grape and the Glass

Oh grape, you sly little fellow,
You tickle taste buds, bright and yellow.
In the glass, a swirl of cheer,
Come one, come all, let's drink and jeer!

Sloshing laughter fills the air,
Why does the cork avoid the fair?
Because it knows, with every sip,
With friends around, we cannot trip!

Moondrops on the Vineyard Path

Under moonlight, shadows chase,
Wine in hand, the night's a race.
We stumble here, we giggle there,
Who knew grapes could lead to dare?

Lost in laughter, tipsy fun,
Shining stars above us run.
The path is winding, oh what a caper,
Let's nap in vines, then wake for paper!

Aromatic Dreams in the Cellar

In shadows deep, where barrels rest,
A cork popped loud, it's quite the jest!
A grape once shy, now full of cheer,
Whispers sweet secrets to me, my dear.

The bottles giggle, the labels dance,
As I sip slowly, lost in a trance.
They claim to know the vintage lore,
While I just wait for the next encore.

Mosaic of the Maturing Fruit

Brighter than sunlight, the fruits do tease,
Bouncing around like they're at ease.
A grape in a hat, another in shoes,
Each fruit with a story, none with the blues.

They chat and they laugh under leaves so bright,
Confessing their crushes by moonlight.
The clusters are mingling, quite a sight to see,
With each little drop, there's glee and esprit.

Celebrating the Crush

In the crush of the moment, all stomp with glee,
Juice flying high, what a slippery spree!
With a laugh and a slip, down someone goes,
Grape juice fountains, oh how it flows!

The fermenters groove, adding to the cheer,
Whispering fizz, saying, 'We're nearly here!'
Pandalicious chaos, laughter on repeat,
Grapes breakdance, this party's a treat.

Harvesting Heartstrings

With baskets in hand, we dance through the rows,
Filling them up as the chuckle grows.
Each grape we pluck sings a merry tune,
Under the watchful eye of the moon.

A neighbor's cat joins, chasing shadows wide,
As we gather, laughter takes us for a ride.
The harvest is more than just grapes in the bin,
It's friendships and fun that make us all grin.

Echoes of the Fermentation

In barrels we chat, in bubbles we giggle,
The grapes tell tales with a fizzy jiggle.
Fermentation's dance is never so neat,
As we stomp around with our grape-squished feet.

Yeast makes a ruckus, like kids at a fair,
While the wine whispers secrets only we dare.
Oh, the drama that brews in a bottle so round,
Pour it out quick—let good times abound!

Twilight in the Tasting Room

Twilight drapes over our glasses so fine,
Each sip's a story, each clink's a good sign.
With swirling aromas that tickle our noses,
We laugh at the way tasting sometimes exposes.

A swirl, a snort, then a spurt of grape juice,
It's pure comedy—who knew wine was so loose?
Restricted to sips, yet wild on the tongue,
Toasting to friendships forever among.

Nectar of the Ancients

They whisper of ages, our bottles divine,
With flavors as rich as a joke that's benign.
Each sip has our giggles doing cartwheels,
As the cork pops out—oh, the joy that reveals!

The ancients would chuckle, if they saw us today,
Gulping their nectar in such silly play.
With every drop, we're transported in time,
And the silly we feel becomes quite the rhyme.

Rooted Recollections

From roots deep and tangled, we gather our fun,
Remembering where it all was begun.
The stories and laughter grow sweeter with age,
In our goofy remembrance, we fill every page.

We slip on the leaves and tumble in joy,
Play hide and seek with that old corkscrew toy.
With roots that are sturdy, but spirits that soar,
Each moment a vineyard, with laughter galore!

Harvesting Haikus

Grapes bounce in the sun,
Picking turns to a race,
Who knew they'd all run?
Call it a juicy chase.

Sipping while we work,
Juice spills on my shirt,
Grapes laugh at the clumsies,
Turns out, I'm dessert.

Stomping in a line,
Feet squish in the muck,
A toe has now met wine,
It really is bad luck!

Whispers of sweet cheer,
Harvest moons gleam bright,
We're dancing with the dear,
Wine spills, oh what a sight!

Lamentations of the Lost Grape

Oh, my little grape,
You slipped from the vine,
Rolling down the slope,
What an awful sign!

You dreamed of a crush,
To be such fine wine,
But fate made a hush,
Now you're stuck as brine!

Bouncing with great zeal,
You thought it was fate,
But now you're a meal,
Somebody's on a plate!

With friends in despair,
We seek the lost prize,
One grape on a chair,
Makes for soggy pies!

A Symphony of Sunsets

Chardonnay not far,
Sipping near the dusk,
Grapes dream of a jar,
Fruits, wine, and a musk.

Fiddles playing sweet,
As the barrels roll,
Tunes made from our feet,
Grapes dancing, oh so whole!

A trumpet shared a laugh,
While corks pop with glee,
Despite the grape's gaffe,
We still sing with tea.

Sunsets set the scene,
Colors swirling in air,
Memories like a dream,
Grapes know they look fair!

Palettes of the Local Palette

Brushes paint the sky,
With splashes of fine red,
Grapes giggle nearby,
'Is that our future spread?'

Artistry in spills,
Wine stains on the floor,
The scent of lost thrills,
Grapes seek out an encore!

Cheddar greets the brie,
Crackers dance and hum,
Oh, what a jubilee,
As vintners feel dumb!

Palette full of fun,
Cheerful and absurd,
Wine flows like a run,
The best is unheard!

Soft Shadows on the Soil

In the field where shadows play,
The grapes are plotting all day.
"Let's roll down the hill and flee!"
Squeaked a bunch, feeling carefree.

The farmer chased with a frown,
While the grapes giggled, tumbling down.
"We're just having fun, you see!"
Cried a rebel vine, wild and free.

When night falls, they start a ball,
Jazzing it up, having a ball.
With silly moves and grape-sized jokes,
They dance around, those fruity folks.

At dawn, they pretend to be shy,
Nestled close, saying goodbye.
"Just a dream," they often claim,
As the sun rises, igniting the game.

Whispers of the Old Vines

The old vines tell tales of yore,
Of grape fights and naps on the floor.
"We were wild, we were spry!"
Said one to another with a sigh.

"Remember the time we turned to wine?"
"Oh yes! What a buzz, so divine!"
Giggling softly, on wind they drift,
With memories ripe, their spirits lift.

They gossip about the sun's warm rays,
And old cellar pranks from the days.
"That barrel rolled like a wild beast,
And spilled our secrets to the feast!"

A whisper of laughter fills the air,
As they reminisce without a care.
"We're the legends of this land,
And none could ever understand!"

Grapes in the Gloaming

In the gloaming, the grapes convene,
Sharing secrets, acting mean.
"Don't squish me!" one yelled in fright,
"I'm not ready for the harvest night!"

They fashioned hats from leafy greens,
Organizing mock beauty scenes.
"I'll be the queen, and you shall bow!"
"You? Oh please! You look like a cow!"

Twilight hung thick, laughter flowed,
Rolling around, their fun overflowed.
"Bet I can dodge the farmer's hand!"
And off they go, a wild band!

As stars peep through with a grin,
These grapes laugh at all they win.
Under moonlight's watchful gaze,
They frolic through their grape-filled days.

The Sweetness of Time

Time rolls sweet like the finest wine,
With every drop, life's moments shine.
"A toast!" they cheer, as skies turn blue,
"To the good times, and friendships true!"

They debate which way the wind will blow,
And if tomorrow's sun will show.
"Better shine bright, or we'll melt!"
Said a cheeky grape, laughter felt.

With thoughts of sugar, spice, and fun,
They plan to play until they run.
"Let's prank the farmer, it's our fate!"
They cackle with delight, oh, it's great!

As days turn to seasons, they unite,
Creating stories by moonlight.
In this sweet game of wrinkled foes,
They savor life, as the laughter grows.

The Grape's Farewell

In rows so fine, the grapes would bide,
They tried to run, oh what a ride!
With tiny feet, they danced around,
But soon they found their crush profound.

A party planned, the leaves a-flare,
The harvest dance beyond compare.
With silly hats and juice to sip,
They waved goodnight, a grape's last trip.

The miller grinned, his tools in hand,
Said, "Come on, friends, we've got a plan!"
They laughed and giggled, ready to roll,
In barrels deep, to lose control.

As bottles popped and laughter soared,
The grape's farewell, they all adored.
In vine-clad dreams, they took their leave,
With juice-drenched hearts, they'd never grieve.

Chardonnay Dreams

On sunny days, the chardonnay gleamed,
With visions of wine, they all dreamed.
They called for rain, the clouds complied,
Dancing in puddles, oh how they pried!

They whispered tales of fancy flights,
Of family dinners and swirling nights.
With every sip, they twirled in grace,
Stumbling home in a grape-hued race.

In glasses raised, the cheers echoed loud,
A clumsy crew, but joy was proud.
They laughed at spills, they chuckled near,
For every drop brought shining cheer.

As evening fell, dreams took their course,
Grapes held hands, unleashed their force.
In dreams they danced, oh what a thrill,
A chardonnay wish — it's never nil!

Autumn's Embrace

In the golden light of autumn's grace,
The grapes wore sweaters, a cozy embrace.
With leaves that danced, a colorful spree,
They gathered for laughter, oh what a glee!

They played hide and seek among the vine,
Chasing the sun, feeling divine.
With crunching underfoot, they pranced about,
Silly little grapes, there's never a doubt!

As crunching apples joined the fun,
Grapes did their best but outran none.
With cider's cheer, they'd spin and sway,
In autumn's arms, they'd laugh and play.

The harvest moon, a beacon bright,
Encouraged grapes to party all night.
As shadows danced, they sang with cheer,
In autumn's embrace, they found their beer!

Starlit Rows

Under the stars, the rows did glisten,
The grapes giggled loud, they had to listen.
With a wink and a smile, they twinkled bright,
Toasting the moon in a fanciful night.

They whispered secrets of love and old,
Of vines entangled, a story bold.
With every pop of a corked bottle,
They laughed and sang, no need to throttle.

In starlit rows, they danced with flair,
Grapes on the move, in moonlit air.
Their laughter soared, a silly spree,
A grape-tastic tale, wild and free.

As night wore thin, the crickets played,
The grape brigade, they'd never fade.
In starlit rows, the memories grew,
A wild grape party, just me and you.

Brooding Beneath the Boughs

In the shade where grapes do grow,
A squirrel is running to and fro.
I thought I'd sit, just take my ease,
But here comes trouble, buzzing bees!

They think I'm sweet like fruit so ripe,
With every buzz, they swipe and swipe.
I swat and laugh, what a fine chase,
Next time, I'll bring my picnic space!

The sun is hot, it hits like bricks,
I sip my juice, with crunchy bits.
The grape must have a funny trick,
It made my jig a stumbly kick!

I thought I'd brood, just ponder life,
But ended up in silly strife.
With grapes above, and bees about,
I fear this fun, I'm ready to shout!

Scale of the Sweetness

I weighed my grapes upon a scale,
Their sweetness made my face turn pale.
For every ounce, I lost my pride,
As munchy munchers came to hide!

They climbed the fence, these chubby things,
In search of juicy, luscious rings.
With every nibble, they conspire,
My fun snacks, they lit on fire!

What's this I see, a weighty prize?
A batch so bright, it blinds the eyes.
I pick a bunch, and what a sigh,
They're gone! Oh dear, they made me cry!

But sweet defeat is bittersweet,
I'll laugh it off with fun to eat.
For what's a harvest, after all,
If no one's here to sing and sprawl?

Verses in the Vineyard

Amidst the vines, I hear a cheer,
A grape-tastic party's near!
The cups will clink, the laughter flow,
As funny tales begin to grow.

I wore a hat, that soared so high,
It scared a bird right from the sky.
With every sip, I thought of schemes,
Yet snoozed instead, in wild dreams!

The grapes around began to dance,
And offered me a chance, a chance!
I stumbled forth with lack of grace,
Then joined the rabble, joined the race!

In silly glee, we tossed the fruit,
Though some got squished, they didn't mute.
With laughter ripe and joy in store,
I'll plant more fun, and maybe four!

Reflections Beneath the Arbor

Under the boughs of leafy shade,
I thought I'd nap, but plans have strayed.
A laughing pup has found my hat,
He prances round in gleeful spat!

With each attempt to snag my cap,
I spin like grapes in silly trap.
The dog goes wild, a little blur,
And I just giggle, what a stir!

The fruits above, they wink and tease,
As squirrels play tunes upon the breeze.
I join the jam with claps and hums,
And dance along, despite the thumps!

So here's my dance, a code of fun,
With every twirl, I've surely won.
Beneath the arbor, life is bright,
With laughter ringing through the night!

A Toast to the Terroir

Raise a glass to the dirt, so fine,
Where grapes play tag and dance in line.
They laugh as they ripple in the sun,
With every sip, let the giggles run.

In barrels they whisper, tales untold,
Of mice who dream of riches, bold.
Beneath the corks, there's quite a cheer,
As corks pop off, let joy draw near.

The wine's so sweet, it makes us grin,
With fruity notes of mischief in.
Each toast we make, the laughter grows,
In every drop, a funny prose.

So let us toast to this grand affair,
Where grapes are kings and we're all laid bare.
A little spill, a little cheer,
In every glass, a world sincere.

Blossoms Beneath the Bough

Underneath the boughs, we find a show,
With flowers chatting just below.
Petals gossip, bees in a spin,
While critters plot a garden win.

A squirrel's up to give a toast,
While butterflies debate the host.
Rabbits hop and stomp with glee,
In this circus, no one can see!

With bees in bonnets, buzzing around,
Each blossom laughs, a joyful sound.
The sun peeks in with a wink and grin,
For nature's fun is where we begin.

So let's embrace this chaos bright,
With every bloom, a new delight.
In colorful chaos, we find our song,
In blossoms' light, we all belong.

The Language of Leaves

Leaves are chattering between the trees,
Whispering jokes carried by the breeze.
With every flutter, a funny tale,
Of squirrels in hats who set the sail.

They giggle and rustle as winds may sway,
With secret plots for a leafy play.
A dandelion, posed like a star,
Claims to be the funniest by far.

As sunlight tickles each green face,
The foliage dances in a wild chase.
Spinning around with leaves on the ground,
In this merry talk, joy is profound.

So when you wander through shades of green,
Listen closely for the laughs unseen.
For in every leaf that sways on high,
There's a chuckle waiting—oh my, oh my!

Vine-Lined Chronicles

Once upon a vine, stories unfold,
Of grapes who dream beyond a mold.
In shadowy corners, they slink and play,
With monsters of market keeping at bay.

The goblet grins with a liquid tale,
As glasses clink and giggles sail.
Every swirl whispers secrets so grand,
Of grape-juice capers, oh did you understand?

With every sip, a plot thickens fast,
As shades of blush and ruby are cast.
They're plotting to prank that bottle of red,
While bubbles rise up with mischief ahead.

So gather your friends, raise your cheer,
To chronicles shared without any fear.
In vine-lined adventures, let's all partake,
For every glass brought the smiles we make.

The Winemaker's Muse

In a barrel, dreams do stew,
With grapes that giggle, laugh, and coo,
The corked ideas pop with cheer,
While the wine seems toage—Oh dear!

A splash of fun in every pour,
As bottles dance upon the floor,
Grape juice whispers silly rhymes,
And even corks can change with times.

When feet are stomped, it's quite the sight,
To see those grapes in sheer delight,
A vintage joke will surely steep,
And laughter spills as others weep.

So raise your glass and toast with glee,
For winemaking's pure jubilee,
In every sip, a chuckle hides,
While drunken grapes roll with pride.

Dances of Decanting

The bottle wobbles, full and round,
As laughter echoes all around,
We give a swirl, we give a twirl,
And watch the wine begin to whirl.

A twist of wrist, a joyous fling,
Decanting's such a silly thing,
The wine leaps high, the cork takes flight,
As we toast to the silliest night.

With every splash, the fun ignites,
A battle of the grape delights,
The glasses clink, a bubbly tune,
While grapes perform beneath the moon.

As laughter flows, we'll drink and sing,
For every pour's a joyous fling,
And in this dance, we find our bliss,
With every sip, we steal a kiss.

A Symphony of Tannins

With grapes in hand, we start the show,
A symphony of zesty flow,
Each berry sings a funny note,
As tannins dance on everyone's throat.

The conductor waves—a cork in sight,
As we toast to pure delight,
The wine notes wobble, then take flight,
A grape parade, oh what a sight!

In the cellars, laughter blends,
With barrels rolling, making friends,
Giggles echo in the cask,
As we toast to the fun we ask.

From every sip, a chuckle swells,
With humorous stories everyone tells,
As tannins tickle, no need to pout,
In our melange, we twirl about.

Odes to Old Oak

The old oak barrels creak with zest,
In every grain, a secret fest,
They whisper tales of past and fun,
As lovers of the grape have run.

With every sip, a giggle near,
Old wood enhances every cheer,
In their embrace, we find a laugh,
As wine flows well, our hearts do quaff.

An oak's embrace is warm and bright,
It cradles bubbles in the night,
As corks pop loud, and spirits soar,
In this aged wood, we all adore.

So raise a glass to timeless cheer,
As laughter echoes, loud and clear,
In odes to oak, with spirits high,
We toast our joy—oh me, oh my!

The Vintage Echo

In the rows where grapes do sway,
A vine once told me, "Hey, no pay!"
The sun is hot, the wine's a bit sour,
But laughter blooms like a bright flower.

When harvest time begins the fuss,
We joke that wine's made just for us.
With buckets full and spills galore,
We'll dance 'til we can't take no more!

Each sip brings tales of silly days,
Of clumsy feet and grape-stained ways.
So raise a glass, let spirits flow,
In the vintage echo, laughter grows.

So cheers to those who tip and spill,
With every drop, a laugh to thrill.
We toast to friends, both near and far,
And hope our jokes won't go too far!

A Dance of Clusters

In the field where laughter blooms,
The grapes giggle in their plumes.
Dancing clusters in a row,
They sway like friends at a show.

With every stomp upon the floor,
The juice just leaps, we laugh for more.
Oh, tripping is the norm today,
As we swirl and twirl, hip-hip-hooray!

The casks are full, the bounty sweet,
But watch your step – mind your feet!
For while we sip and sing our song,
Funny tales just can't go wrong.

So gather 'round, you merry crew,
With every glass, we start anew.
A toast to friends and grape-filled skies,
In this silly dance, our laughter flies!

When Vines Embrace the Sky

When vines stretch high, they whisper low,
"Look at us! We're the stars of the show!"
As clouds roll by, they try to climb,
But grapes just giggle, feeling sublime.

The sun, he grins – oh so bright,
While we take sips, our hearts take flight.
With each light laugh, and silly cheer,
The winemaker spills more than just beer!

Dancing with seeds, under the blue,
We'll toast to all that we pursue.
For as the vines embrace the air,
Our laughter bubbles everywhere!

So raise your glass, don't hesitate,
In our sweet fields, it's never late.
For when the day turns to night,
We'll gather here, laughing in delight!

Cellar Secrets Unveiled

In the cellar where shadows sigh,
A grape once winked and said, "Oh my!"
Secrets tucked in barrels tight,
We giggle at the goofy sight.

Each cork a tale, each bottle's dream,
Of silly quirks that make us beam.
We pop a cap, and with a cheer,
The neighbors wonder what's going here!

With every pour, the jokes do flow,
"Is it the wine or just the glow?"
The vintage laughs, they dance and prance,
Making even corks, lose their stance!

So raise your glass in hidden halls,
We'll drink to fun and silly falls.
For in this cellar's wobbly fate,
Laughter ages, never waits!

The Wine-Touched Wordsmith

A wordsmith pours his jug, oh dear,
He spills his thoughts, they disappear.
With grape-stained hands and tipsy rhymes,
He crafts fine tales in chaotic times.

His muse is drunk, she slurs and sways,
As laughter bubbles in the sun's warm rays.
Each line a sip, each laugh a cheer,
His stories grow as we chug our beer.

Quips of corks and playful puns,
As wobbly thoughts become sweet runs.
A hiccup here, a giggle there,
His bottles corked with playful air.

At dusk, he twirls, a dance so grand,
With bottles clinking, wine glass in hand.
He toasts to life, with a funny twist,
A wordsmith's joy, you can't resist!

Aromas from the Past

Through scents of grapes, we reminisce,
About those times we raised a hiss.
With every cork that pops awake,
Old stories come, new laughs they make.

A whiff of dirt, the squish of grapes,
We chuckle loud, in merry shapes.
Remember when we spilled the wine?
That carpet stain still feels divine!

The vintage jokes still linger sweet,
Like sticky fingers and bare feet.
With every sip, we surge ahead,
And weave our tales, a grape-filled thread.

We clink our glasses, toast to fate,
Each memory rich, never too late.
Odd aromas swirl and dance,
In every drop, a joyful chance!

Harmonies of the Harvest

In fields of gold, we hum a tune,
With grapes a-dancing, beneath the moon.
The harvest shouts, a chorus loud,
As tipsy jokes draw in a crowd.

The crunch of leaves, the squish of wine,
We laugh and twirl, it's harvest time!
With baskets full and smiles wide,
We joyously stomp with grape-filled pride.

There's harmony in every step,
With grape-stains marking where we've wept.
For every fall, there's laughter's flow,
As nature's rhythm steals the show.

With each soft note, a bottle's pop,
We sing out loud, we'll never stop.
Through seasons bright, with jokes entwined,
In every crush, true joy we find!

Beyond the Barrel's Edge

A barrel rolls, it starts to sway,
As silly secrets spill and play.
With laughter round it rocks and teeters,
The world turns giddy on grape-filled meters.

Behind the barrel, jokes collide,
A vintage comedy we can't hide.
The wine spills forth, like laughter's cheer,
Each drop a giggle, loud and clear.

Oh, what a mess, what glorious fun,
As corks go popping—here comes the sun!
In dribbles and spills, we find our song,
With friends beside, it won't be long.

For every sip beyond the edge,
We craft our tales, we make our pledge.
To laugh, to sip, and playful shout,
With every barrel, joy's about!

The Gathering in the Grove

Underneath the leafy shade,
We gather, friends and drink parade.
With laughter bouncing off the trees,
And jokes that float upon the breeze.

The ants join in, a tiny crew,
While squirrels eye our snacks, it's true!
Bottles clink, and giggles burst,
In this fine grove, we quench our thirst.

The sun dips low, the jokes turn tall,
We pick each other, one and all.
The punchlines land with grape-filled cheer,
As we toast to another year!

When evening falls, we'll dance and sway,
In this little grove where we love to play.
With hearts so light, and spirits bright,
Our gathering remains a joyful night.

Liquid Sunshine Reflections

Gold flows freely in our glasses,
Velvety dreams, the world it amasses.
We sip that sunlight, oh so divine,
As the cork pops, we laugh and whine.

A splash on shirts, they joke, oh dear!
"Is that a stain or a souvenir?"
Bubbles fizz and giggles roar,
As we ponder what's behind that door.

The corkscrew dances in my hand,
While friends unite to share a brand.
With each pour, we spill some lore,
As tales unfold of wines and more.

Let's raise a glass, toast to our fate,
For memories steeped in fun, they rate!
So here's to laughter, love, and cheer,
In liquid sunshine, year after year.

Grapevine Confessions

Among the leaves, our secrets flow,
Between the vines, we share and glow.
With giggles wrapped in liquid fate,
We confess our sins, it's never late.

"I drank too much!" one says with glee,
While another giggles, "No, not me!"
The vines all lean in, they want to hear,
Our playful tales mixed with good cheer.

The grapes, they eavesdrop, oh so sly,
As we fret, complain and vie.
With every sip, our worries blend,
Turning to laughter with each new friend.

The night grows warm, our hearts align,
In these grape confessions, we drink, we dine.
So raise your glass, and let it be known,
With every burden, we're not alone!

Rhyme in the Rackhouse

Deep in the cellar, the barrels roll,
A rhyme escapes from deep in the soul.
Each barrel whispers, tales untold,
Of grapes turned gold and friendships bold.

A tipple here, a chuckle there,
The rackhouse hums with tales to share.
We rhyme the night with tipsy glee,
As corks fly high, just wait and see!

"The wine's so good!" one cheerful bard,
"My head will spin, but I'm not marred!"
With every sip, we rhyme and dance,
In this rackhouse, we take our chance.

A toast to fun and silly schemes,
Where every laugh becomes a dream.
In the rackhouse, we find our muse,
With laughter and rhyme the soul will choose.

Elegy of the Enduring Roots

In a garden where grapes once grew,
The weeds have staged a grand debut.
They dance and twirl, such silly sights,
As sunlight fades on summer nights.

With roots that snicker underground,
They plot to make mischief abound.
The wine's on hold, they'll make a toast,
To all the things that matter most.

The jester worms in purple skin,
Have taken up the puns within.
While fruit could boast of grander schemes,
It's laughter now that fills the dreams.

So here's to roots of every guise,
In this odd patch of earth that lies.
For while the grapes may take their leave,
The jokes remain, and we believe.

Gleanings from the Grape

Oh gather round, ye grape enthusiasts,
Let's ponder on our juicy fuss.
These little spheres in clusters cling,
In harvest time, oh how they sing!

They wrinkle up in sunny heat,
And lay about—now isn't that neat?
With squished-up juice and sticky hands,
We toast to life, in giggly bands.

Like bowling balls with skins so fine,
We roll them out—our grape design.
The drinks we make from silly sips,
Spill laughter out from all our lips.

So raise your glass, and don't be shy,
For grapes will never tell you why.
We find our joy in every peel,
In every sip, oh, what a thrill!

Spheres of the Sommelier

A sommelier with a flair for jest,
Holds court in wine, he's surely blessed.
With glasses clinked and laughter high,
He tells us tales that float on by.

He sniffs the bottle, with a grin,
And spins a yarn with just a spin.
"Oh, this red's from my auntie's vine,
Confirmed by grape, not grape divine."

The crowd erupts, then falls in awe,
As he sips red with a teasing jaw.
"Hints of laughter, with notes of cheer,
And finish strong, the punchline here!"

So when you're stuck in wine's fine dance,
Call on the sommelier's chance.
For laughter pours in every glass,
In every drop, the moments pass.

Beyond the Bottle

Beyond the bottle, stories burst,
Of tipsy tales and drunken thirst.
Each cork pops joy, a happy sound,
As laughter flies and troubles drown.

The merlot whispers secrets old,
Of love lost bright and dreams retold.
Each sip unveils a fresh new ride,
Where whimsy reigns, and hearts abide.

With glasses raised, the puns take flight,
As we toast to joys that feel just right.
The bubbles giggle with every fizz,
In this fine hour, we live like whiz.

So leave your worries, take a chance,
And join the fun, come join the dance.
For every drop with laughter we borrow,
Turns ordinary nights to bright tomorrow.

Palette of Harvest Artistry

In the grape-stomping race, how we dance,
With squished toes and giggles, not a chance!
Pallets of purple paint on our feet,
Artistry born from a fruity retreat.

A splash of red here, a drizzle of white,
Looking like artists, what a comical sight!
With every step, we create a new hue,
Masterpieces made from grape juice and goo.

Bottles are laughing, corks twist with glee,
Who's the next victim for wine tasting spree?
Swirling our glasses with playful delight,
Artistry sips under the moonlight.

So raise your glass high and spill with grace,
Laughter and chaos, a beautiful mess to embrace!
With the harvest in hand and joy in the air,
Palette of laughter, memories to share.

The Savor of Serenity

In a bottle of bliss, we clink with our crew,
Each sip a reminder, life's better in view.
Sunset's warm glow on our cheeks, oh so bright,
Savoring moments, what a silly sight!

Out in the fields, with grapes on our hats,
Worrying less about troublesome chats.
With each pour, we chuckle, we spill, we cheer,
Serenity comes from a grape juice-filled beer.

The cheese tastes better when laughter's the spread,
Who knew pairing joy could be so widespread?
A picnic so jolly, beneath the old tree,
With friends and good wine, oh it's heavenly!

So toast to the silly, to the joy, to the fun,
With every sip, we forget what we've done.
Embrace all the flavor, let giggles take flight,
In this savor of madness, everything's right.

Wine's Woven Stories

In bottles reside tales of laughter and cheer,
With every sip taken, a memory near.
From grapes on the vine to a cork in the sky,
Wine's woven stories will always fly high.

A tale of a grape that rolled too far,
Ended up sleeping beneath a big star.
With snickers and bubbles that rise with the pour,
Every glass tells a story, oh what a score!

Swirl it, sniff it, and dive in with zest,
Who knew a drink could turn us to jest?
In vineyards of folly, where grapes often play,
Turned into giggles at the end of the day.

So, pour out the laughter, each sip a new plot,
Each bottle a chapter, a miracle shot.
With tales that unfold, as we lift up our glass,
Wine's stories of joy are never to pass.

Sun-Kissed Elegance

Under the sun, with a glass in hand,
We strut like we're models on fine golden sand.
With hats a bit crooked and smiles so wide,
Sun-kissed elegance beams, oh what a ride!

Dancing with shadows while sipping our best,
Who knew that grapes could lead to such zest?
A splash of the bubbly, we twirl in delight,
In this silly soirée, everything feels right.

The sun may be setting, but spirits are high,
With laughter that echoes and jokes that fly by.
A toast to the clumsy, the splendid, the bold,
Sun-kissed elegance, worth its weight in gold.

So gather your friends, share a giggle or two,
As we bask in the warmth of a sky so blue.
With joy pouring forth like a fine vintage red,
In this whimsical moment, all worries are shed.

Essence in Elysium

In a land where grapes love to dance,
Cork pops like a chance romance.
Barrels roll down the hill with glee,
Chasing one another, just wait and see!

The sun gets tipsy, just like the must,
Giggles arise from the grapevine's crust.
A bee buzzes loudly, joins in the cheer,
As vines whisper secrets we're meant to hear.

Bottles wear hats, they're dressed to the nines,
Laughing together as corks break lines.
In this silly land where grapes take flight,
We raise our glasses and toast to the night!

So let us sit back, let the laughter flow,
In this grape-infused realm where silliness grows.
With every sip, a chuckle abounds,
In this joyful place where humor resounds!

Vignettes of the Vines

In a garden where fermentation sings,
Grapes wear sneakers, oh what fun it brings!
They race each other, up and down the row,
Stumbling and tumbling, putting on a show.

The winemaker's cat thinks he's in charge,
Sipping the juice, living quite large.
The guard dog howls, but he's on the side,
Dreaming of grapes on a merry ride!

Seagulls steal grapes, thinking they rule,
As the farmer chuckles, "What a fine fool!"
A picnic unfolds with a laugh and a game,
Each sip brings giggles, nothing's the same!

So raise up your glass, let the tales unwind,
In this playful patch where joy's defined.
With every laugh shared under the sun,
Vignettes of the vines make life so fun!

Stardust in the Decanter

Underneath the stars, where the grapes tell tales,
The moon joins in, with glimmering trails.
The merlot's giggling, the cabernet sways,
As we sip on dreams in merry displays.

The decanter sparkles, like a gala at night,
Winking and nodding, it's quite the sight!
The cheese plate dances, with crackers in tow,
All join the fest, in a playful glow.

A sprightly cork jumps, it springs from the bottle,
Landing right near us, looking noble.
"This party is grand, let's dance till we drop!"
With laughter as our music, we'll never stop!

So here's to the spirit that gleefully flows,
In this starlit garden where mirth always grows.
Let's fill up our glasses, toast to the night,
With stardust in decanters, everything's right!

Nectar for the Soul

In a field of grapes where humor is spun,
Each crush brings giggles and endless fun.
Grape jellybeans tumble down in delight,
As the sun drops low, painting the night.

Wine glasses chatter, exchanging their jokes,
While vintage corks giggle with all of the folks.
A silly old barrel starts rolling away,
"Catch me if you can!" it's yelling in play!

The harvest moon fuels this whimsical brew,
As we toast to the foolish, the old, and the new.
With pride we sip, feeling whole and alive,
For laughter's the nectar—forever we thrive!

So dance with the grapes, let the fun unfold,
In this silly world, there's laughter to hold.
With every sweet sip, our spirits take flight,
Nectar for the soul, we laugh through the night!

Garden of Bottles

In a garden where grapes grow stout,
Bottles roll in and out,
The corks pop like happy pranks,
As the wine flows down the ranks.

One ladybug sips wine with flair,
While vines do a wobbly air,
A squirrel steals a bottle's shine,
Claiming he's the king of the vine.

The hangovers hang like old coats,
While the birds join in on happy hoats,
Drunk on nectar, they sing real loud,
Reminding us they've grown quite proud.

So here we toast to garden fun,
Where each bottle shines like the sun,
With giggles bubbling in every glass,
Cheers to the grapes, let the laughter last!

Grapevine Chronicles

Once lived a vine with tales so tall,
Of grapes that danced and sang at hall,
A bit ofmischief, a lot of fun,
Sipping sunshine 'til the day is done.

The gophers plotted secret schemes,
They swiped the grapes and stole the dreams,
While rabbits played a game of hide,
In the merry fruit festival, they'd take pride.

One grape named Fred claimed to be wise,
With jokes so cheesy, they'd mesmerize,
He cracked a laugh with every squish,
While we all blushed at his funny wish.

So gather 'round and share the glee,
In these chronicles of a wild spree,
With every sip, let's laugh away,
Until the sun sets on the day!

Roots of Resilience

Deep in the muck, the roots they grew,
With dreams of grapes in morning dew,
Through storms and sun, they stood so bold,
Their stories told like wine turned gold.

The earthworms dance, a wriggly crew,
Reciting tales, both old and new,
Of shenanigans beneath the ground,
Where joy and laughter can abound.

A single root claims a seat at the bar,
With wine glass high, saying, 'Look at my scar!'
They toast to survival, to pranks and nooks,
In this haven of humor—just read the books!

So here's to the roots, though tangled and twined,
With laughter and vines, they're perfectly aligned,
In this rich soil, resilience grows,
Like the laughter that only a vineyard knows!

Lush Layers

In a lush landscape, layers unfold,
Like stories of grapes, both funny and bold,
A parrot squawks jokes from the leafy lane,
While frogs hop in, bringing joy and pain.

Beneath the vines, secrets deep,
Where snails argue and bumblebees leap,
Every layer holds laughter inside,
In this garden of joy, there's nowhere to hide.

And a wise old owl keeps watch from above,
As the grapes spin tales of mischief and love,
Each berry boasts a giggle or two,
As we all gather 'round for a drink or a brew.

So let's celebrate all that's lush and bright,
With layers of laughter, our spirits take flight,
In this patch of happiness, we share a toast,
To the funny follies we cherish the most!

Sipping the Seasons

With grapes as friends, we raise our glass,
To seasons changing, oh how they pass!
Harvest moon shines, our laughter flows,
Who knew wine could cure all woes?

The summer sun, it tries so hard,
To plump the grapes in backyard yard.
But winter's chill, it sneaks right in,
Then slips on ice - oh what a sin!

Autumn's charm, we all adore,
With scarves and snuggles, who needs more?
But spilled some wine on grandma's lap,
We laugh and call it a cozy nap!

So here we sit with bottles bright,
Sipping seasons deep into the night.
With friends by side, let's toast the year,
In grape-filled bliss and childish cheer!

Notes in the Bunch

The grapes on vines sing songs untold,
With cheeky grins, they're brave and bold.
They jiggle and dance with each sweet breeze,
Oh, don't they know? They're meant to please!

Along comes Fred, with his straw hat,
He swears he knows the best grape chat.
But as he trips, we all just see,
Those winner wines, they flee with glee!

Sipping songs that float above,
Like silly whispers with hints of love.
In every bunch, a note rings clear,
Life's a joke, and we're the cheer!

So raise your glass, let laughter spring,
From grapes that laugh, and us that sing.
In every sip, a tale so fun,
Cheers to the grapes, and everyone!

Fabled Fields

In fabled fields where antics thrived,
The grapes conspired, they all connived.
To leap and twirl in rows so neat,
They giggled, 'We're a lucky treat!'

Farmer Joe, with his silly hat,
Could never tell the good grapes from that!
Yet every time he took a sip,
He'd lose his shoes - a funny trip!

The ladies came with laughter loud,
To find the ripest in the crowd.
But as they picked, they tripped in glee,
Falling 'neath the grape's spree!

So here we laugh in golden light,
In fabled fields, all feels just right.
With each clink of glass, we bubble and cheer,
Life's a vine, let's hold it dear!

Clusters of Time

In clusters of time, we dance a jig,
With every sip, we don't need a fig.
The past comes back with a silly grin,
As memories float like breezes spin.

Old vintage tales we laugh about,
Like ducks in line - they're all around!
When barrels rolled, and corks went pop,
We swirled our troubles - oh what a flop!

Time tricks us, with its little game,
We toast to grapes who feel the same.
With a wink and nudge, they give a shout,
"Let's drink it all, and never pout!"

So hold your glass and make a toast,
To clusters of time, we love the most.
We'll laugh, we'll sing, through thick and thin,
In grape-filled moments, let the fun begin!

The Essence of Earth

In the fields where grapes do grow,
A squirrel steals my snack, you know.
I chase him 'round, we spin and twirl,
Amidst the vines, a silly whirl.

The soil's rich, but so is the jest,
Each slosh of wine's a goofy quest.
I trip and stumble, laugh 'til it hurts,
As mud splatters my favorite shirt.

The wind sings low, it sways the leaves,
I toast to mischief, no one believes.
A cork pops loud, wine spills with grace,
Let's blame the grapes for this wild race!

So raise a glass to the twisty fate,
Every grape has its time, don't wait!
With laughter, love, and zooming bees,
This earth, my friend, is quite the tease!

Serendipity in the Sips.

In a glass of red as I take a sip,
I see a duck with a drunken dip.
Waddling near, it quacks a tune,
While I just giggle beneath the moon.

Bottles stacked like a high school stack,
With labels stuck just a little whack.
I pour too much, it froths and spills,
Who needs a beach when you've got thrills?

Grapes dance around in my fuzzy mind,
Castles of grapes, oh how they unwind!
I trip on roots, but I brush it off,
No crocodile tears, just a hearty scoff.

So here's to laughs and silly blunders,
In every sip, the joy it thunders.
Raise your glass, join the bubbly cheer,
In every sip, let's toast without fear!

Grapes of Whispered Dreams

Under the arbor, secrets fly,
Grapes whisper tales as I stroll by.
One grape giggles, "You never knew!"
The other shouts, "Shhh! I see you too!"

A jester's cap hangs on the vine,
I pluck it gently, it tastes like wine.
With sneeze and cough, I'm drenched in red,
Grapes laugh loudly as I shake my head.

The sun dips low, it paints the skies,
While clowns dance 'neath the grape-studded highs.
Each sip, a story, oh so absurd,
Frogs join the fun; they leap and heard!

With every laughter, the harvest gleams,
In mugs of warmth, we toast our dreams.
So gather around, let the fervor seam,
In jests and joy, we sip and beam!

Harvest Moon Serenade

The harvest moon begins to rise,
As I trip over grapes, oh what a prize!
A jolly old toad croaks out a tune,
While shadows dance beneath the moon.

In the cellar, I try to find,
A bottle lost — oh, it's wine unkind!
I laugh at my silliness, what a show,
As I knock over barrels like dominoes.

The night is ripe, but I sing off-key,
With grapes as my backup, how could it be?
We swirl around, create our own beat,
With every sip, we bounce on our feet.

Raise a glass to the whacky delight,
For laughter and wine make everything right.
Under the harvest moon's gentle glow,
Let's dance and toast to the joy we sow!

Hymn of the Hallowed Hills

The grapes are having a party tonight,
They giggle and dance in the soft moonlight.
A cork popped loud, what a silly sight,
Cheers erupted with all their might!

The farmer tripped over his big toe,
Chasing after a runaway flow.
With a splash, the grape juice went to and fro,
Laughter echoed, stealing the show.

A chicken in boots joins the fun,
Twirling around, she thinks she's the one.
While the goats make a mess on the run,
The hills are alive, oh what a pun!

So raise your glass to this merry spree,
To hills that are hallowed and filled with glee.
With every sip, just let it be,
A good time waits for you and me!

Whispers from the Wineglass

In a glass so large, secrets unfold,
The whispers of grapes, stories retold.
"Who dropped the cork?" in chimes bold,
We laugh as we sip, feeling quite old.

A vintage so fine, with bubbles that pop,
One little sip, then off like a hop!
As the room starts to spin and we flop,
The jokes flow freely, and laughter won't stop.

A toast to the grapes, so round and so grand,
With squished feet, they have taken a stand.
The wine flows like rivers, oh isn't it planned?
Just watch your pour or it may get out of hand!

In laughter and cheer, our hearts softly sway,
Each gulp a trip down the funny lane way.
"Another round?" we all shout, "Hooray!"
And the world just melts, a whimsical play!

Melodies in the Meadow

In the meadow a melody starts to play,
With crickets that dance at the end of the day.
A cow sings a tune in a quite funny way,
While the sun dips low, turning night into gray.

Grapes sway with glee, in a sweet little band,
A chorus of berries, united they stand.
The breeze joins in, lending a hand,
Making music that's silly and far from bland.

A squirrel plays drums on a pinecone so fine,
Two birds join in, singing, oh, what a line!
A rabbit jumps high, on a whim, so divine,
As laughter bursts forth, with a glass full of wine.

So dance with the grass, let your worries all fade,
In this meadow of joy, where the fun's never made.
Raise your glass high; there's no need to be swayed,
In melodies sweet, this night we've portrayed!

Refrains of the Rustic Region

In the rustic region where the laughter flows,
Pictures of grapes with the silliest shows.
A pig on a bongo, in shades, how it glows,
With a hiccup of joy, everyone knows!

The moon grins wide at this comical sight,
While sheep do the cha-cha, a whimsical night.
One clumsy goat trips, oh such a delight,
As the joke of the hour, he's quite the insight!

Casks rolling down like a carnival ride,
With a splash and a giggle, we all take a slide.
The wine flows like laughter, it can't be denied,
We're living our best, with the moon as our guide.

So gather your friends for this laughter-filled quest,
In the rustic region, where every night is blessed.
With grapes and with glee, we're crowned as the best,
Raise your glass high, it's a belly laugh fest!

Grapes of Rhyme

In a bunch they tell their tales,
With giggles in the sunny trails.
One grape slips, and there's a squish,
A juicy joke is our birthday wish.

With each sip, they dance and sway,
Their liquid laughter made my day.
The cork pops loud, a vibrant cheer,
Who knew the grapes could be so dear?

A grape in sunglasses, he strikes a pose,
Sipping juice, there's more to those!
The barrels roll, they laugh in glee,
For life's a crush, so come and see!

With every drop, a story brews,
The vineyard's whispers start to amuse.
So raise your glass, let laughter rhyme,
In this fruity world, we toast in time.

Whispers in the Vines

The vines are gossiping today,
Complaining 'bout the sun's bright ray.
"Too hot!" they groan, "We need some shade!"
"Oh please," replied a cluster made.

An ant waltzes, thinks he's grand,
Strutting like he owns the land.
A bumblebee buzzes, full of flair,
"Just zip it, pal! I'm full of air!"

A squirrel drops in, all dressed in green,
"Why just grapes? Let's have a bean!"
The vines all chuckle, "You're quite a sight,
We'll let you party, but don't invite!"

Secrets shared in leafy homes,
They dream of pies, and wine with foams.
In this chatty plot, laughs intertwine,
With all our friends beneath the vine.

Sunlit Harvest

Under the sun, a dance begins,
With grapes on legs, they flip and spin.
One grape trips, and stumbles right,
A giggling cheer, oh what a sight!

With baskets full, we skip and hop,
"Catch me, catch me!" I hear the pop.
The old man chuckles as he leans,
While vines are tangled in morning sheens.

The crew sings out, with voices bright,
A grape-joke here, a pun-filled bite.
As sunlight drips, we dance and play,
"Harvest time's here! Hip-hip-hooray!"

So lift your glass to sunny mirth,
Where laughter crushes all the dearth.
With every sip, the joy ignites,
In this bright harvest, we share delights.

The Cellar's Lament

In the cellar, shadows creep,
The bottles sigh, they're losing sleep.
"Why are we waiting?" they wine and whine,
"Let's pop the cork and feel divine!"

Dust bunnies dance on dusty beams,
They plot to plot their bottle dreams.
A chatty cork: "What's all this fuss?
I've been waiting years, it's a huge plus!"

The barrels grumble, full of age,
"Oh dear, we've turned into sage!"
But together they dream of sweeter times,
Of laughter, libations, and silly rhymes.

With a corkscrew twist, they break the chain,
And in a swirl, they sing the strain.
"Cheers!" they cry, as glasses clink,
In the cellar's heart, they laugh and drink.

Melodies from the Merlot

In the shade of grapes, a tune does play,
Sipping on laughter, we dance and sway.
The corks pop loud, what a joyous sound,
As we spill our tales on the picnic ground.

With each glass lifted, our spirits rise,
A toast to the grapes, and the silly lies.
Each drop's a chuckle, a fit of glee,
We're all tipsy with love, just wait and see.

Beneath the sun, where the laughter flows,
We whine while sipping, while friendship grows.
The grapes all giggle, their secrets shared,
In this vineyard life, no one is scared.

So let's raise our glasses, let the fun unfold,
With Merlot music, our stories told.
In the heart of the vines, we find our cheer,
As grapes become legends, year after year.

A Toast to Dawn

Morning breaks soft, with a mischievous smile,
We sip drowsy dreams; it's been quite a while.
A breakfast of wine, who knew it could be?
With laughter and crumbs, we toast our glee.

The rooster crows loud, the glasses clink,
We cheer for the dawn, and the stains on the sink.
A splash of red, on a pancake stack,
Who needs a filter? Come, join this snack!

The sun's peeking through, with a wink and a nod,
As we spill grape juice, feeling quite odd.
With toasts in the morning, we dance with delight,
The day is young, let's not lose sight!

So here's to the dawn, may it bring us cheer,
With a glass in hand, we conquer our fears.
In this merry hour, let our spirits soar,
Raise your mugs high, there's so much in store!

Echoes Among the Vines

In the whispering leaves, secrets abound,
The grapes have their gossip, they're rumored around.
A jest here, a laugh there, what a fine jest,
These fruity blockbusters put us to the test.

Oh, the tales of the vines, they poke, they tease,
With every sip shared, they tickle with ease.
In the bounteous rows, with sun on our backs,
We giggle and chime, evading the cracks.

With a splash of wine, we become wild folk,
The vines all chuckle, wrap us in smoke.
All the sips shared, create echoes so bright,
In the heart of the vines, we dance through the night.

So join in the fun, don't let it slip by,
The grapes know the way to make spirits fly.
With giggles and grins, we embrace the divine,
Let's echo our cheers, with each tasty vine!

The Tasting Room Tales

Enter the room, with a swirl and a swirl,
The tasting of laughs, let the good times unfurl.
With sips of delight, a story takes flight,
The air's thick with laughter, it feels just right.

A tad too much Riesling, here comes the wit,
Who knew wine could spark such a spirited hit?
As glasses unite, fabrications unfold,
Each story a treasure, a joy to behold.

So pour us some Cabernet, let it just flow,
The fables grow wilder as the barrels glow.
Between sips of joy, and the clinking of glass,
The tales get taller, as moments just pass.

So cap off the night, with a hearty cheer,
In this tasting room, we lose track of fear.
With laughter we linger, our stories entwined,
In our heart of grapes, true friendship we find.

Bottled Sonnets

In bottles lined up, a curious sight,
Each with its story, a hint of delight.
Some promise sweetness, others a funk,
Uncork them with laughter, unleash the junk.

One claims to be bold, a true working man,
Yet tastes like it's had a less-pleasant plan.
With bubbles and giggles, we sip and we cheer,
Who knew that red could feel like a beer?

So let's raise our glasses, toast to the fun,
For nothing pairs better than laughter and rum.
In this vineyard of jokes, we gather with glee,
Chasing corks through the air, like it's meant to be!

Oh, bottles are merry, the moments are bright,
In the glow of the moon, we sip through the night.
With friends and with laughter, we dance and we play,
Life's better with bubbles, let's drink it away!

Vintage Reflections

Grapes in the sun, they giggle and sway,
Wishing they'd come up with something to say.
One whispered, 'I'm Merlot, deep and complex,'
While others just argue, 'Hey, look at my flex!'

The barrels are chatting, they joke all day long,
One thinks he's a hero, the other, a song.
Together they chuckle, their tannins entwined,
With laughs that get deeper as time starts to unwind.

In shadows they whisper, 'Did you hear the last batch?
It tasted quite sour, but nobody snatched.'
The vintner just smiled, he's used to the jest,
He knows that with time, they'll all be at their best.

So raise a glass high to reflections of cheer,
Each bottle a tale worth a giggle or tear.
With laughter and wine, we toast what we share,
For life's a good vintage, so why should we care?

Palette of Passions

In a world of colors, let's paint with wine,
A splash of this Cabernet, that splash divine.
With brushes of laughter, we create a scene,
Staining our shirts, but nobody's mean!

"More bubbles!" one shouts, the canvas erupts,
As sparkle meets color, the pigments corrupt.
A swirl of hilarity, a dash of regret,
Who knew that 'grape stomp' could cause so much sweat?

With laughter like brush strokes, we smear and we blend,
Each glass tells a story, each sip, a new trend.
From blushes of giggles to let's-dance-all-night,
Our palette of passions, so wildly polite.

So pour out your heart in a symphony loud,
With laughter the canvas, be silly and proud.
For every good vintage is best when it's shared,
In this palette of fun, we paint moments, unpaired!

Woven from the Soil

Beneath the rich earth, the grapevines giggle,
As roots intertwine, they start to wiggle.
'Hey, do you recall that storm last fall?
I thought we'd get drowned, like a grape in a brawl!'

In every deep furrow, there's gossip to share,
They whisper sweet secrets, out there in the air.
'You know what I heard? That old oak was a tease!
Telling tales of the race, all the bugs in the breeze.'

But sunshine breaks through, they bask in a glow,
As clusters of joy upon branches do grow.
Harvest brings laughter, a festival fair,
Bottled up friendships, a banquet to share.

So let's toast to the roots that connect us and bind,
With elbows entwined and our quirks all aligned.
For woven from soil, we rise and we play,
Together we flourish, come sip, laugh, and stay!